**Writing Activities
for Students Learning English**

PUT IT IN WRITING

David Blot
and
David M. Davidson

Bronx Community College
City University of New York

Newbury House Publishers, Inc. / Rowley / Massachusetts / 01969

1980

Library of Congress Cataloging in Publication Data

Blot, Dave
  Put it in writing.

  SUMMARY: Suggests topics and exercises and
discusses techniques to help students learn English
through writing.
    1. English language--Text-books for foreigners.
2. English language--Composition and exercises.
[1. English language--Textbooks for foreigners.
2. English language--Composition and exercises]
I. Davidson, David M., joint author.   II. Title.
PE1128.B593   808'.042   80-23208
ISBN 0-88377-175-6

Cover design by Christy Rosso

Photographs on pages 6, 39, 53, 69, 77, 83, 84, 85, and 86 are by Joe Greene

NEWBURY HOUSE PUBLISHERS, INC.

Language Science
Language Teaching
Language Learning

ROWLEY, MASSACHUSETTS 01969

First printing: December 1980
Printed in the U.S.A.   5   4   3   2   1

To Yolanda, Kay and Deborah

and

To the memory of Charles A. Curran

ACKNOWLEDGMENTS

With appreciation to our students whose enthusiasm and progress encouraged us in the development and improvement of the activities that make up this book, and to our colleagues in the Department of Special Educational Services, Bronx Community College, for their helpful suggestions.

CONTENTS

INTRODUCTION

Put It In Writing came into being as a result of the authors' work with college level ESL students at Bronx Community College and also their experience with Charles A. Curran's Counseling-Learning/Community Language Learning Model. The activities in the book go beyond simply being high interest materials. They encourage student investment because they each contain some idea, experience or situation that students value. Students invest themselves because the activity somehow touches them and their lives and therefore they value it. Students write better when the "I" is involved. The "I" can be involved in three ways: 1. When the student writes about himself or herself in, for example, "My Life" or "Chi Lin's Escape to Freedom." 2. When the student writes about another person or event but shows the relationship of that person or event to himself or herself in, for example, "Uncle Carmine" or "The Grocery Store." 3. When the student writes about another person, situation or event that he or she has no relationship to but gets involved in personally because of the values involved. For example, in "Anna and Martin" a student may not be married or, if married, may not be facing the conflict that Anna and Martin are facing, but a female student can value Anna's desire for more independence while a male student can value Martin's position as head of the household.

The value of the dialogues lies in their not being problem-solving activities. The people in the dialogue situations are not problems nor do they have problems for which the students are to supply the answer. They are real people in conflicts for which there may or may not be solutions. For example, in "Anna and Martin" the final statement in students' role playing or dialogue writing sometimes is something to the effect that, "I'm not satisfied. We'll have to talk about this again." Or in "Luisa Rodriguez and Her Mother" an ending sometimes is, "O.K., I'll obey you because you're my mother, but I'm not happy." On the other hand, sometimes partial solutions are found such as when Mrs. Rodriguez suggests that Luisa invite her boyfriend home to dinner or when Martin decides to give up gambling. Sometimes the conflict is resolved

1

completely. To call these dialogue situations "problem-solving" is to miss the point entirely because what engages the students in the dialogue writing are the universal or near universal values explicit and implicit in the situation. For example, love and respect for one's parents or spouse versus the desire for freedom and independence, the desire to live one's own life, to feel worthwhile, etc.

WHO THIS BOOK IS FOR

Put It In Writing was developed over a two and one-half year period and tested over a one year period with community college ESL students. The authors have found that the book is appropriate for students ranging from low intermediate to low advanced in ability. The format and content of the book make it suitable for high school ESL programs, adult ESL community programs and EFL programs as well as for college students.

HOW TO USE THIS BOOK

The approach in some writing books is to teach a point of grammar and then let students practice that grammar in their writing. The writing activity is subordinate to the grammar lesson. However, this book is advocating a different approach, namely, that the students begin with writing. Then, through a combination of correction and follow-up grammar, spelling and vocabulary activities, the students can learn from the mistakes they made in the writing. In other words, the starting point is the self-invested students entering into the writing activity. Their engagement causes them to be more open to and to pay more attention to the help the teacher gives them during and after the writing. They are more open because they value what they are writing and want to do the best they can. What must be understood is that to use this book as the authors intended, the writing must not be perceived by the students as their response to the teacher's grammar lesson. Rather, the grammar, spelling and vocabulary activities must be seen as the teacher's response after the fact to the students' original investment in the writing. Proceeding this way frees the teacher to truly meet the students' needs. While correcting students' writing, the teacher can determine which students need help in spelling, which in grammar, and which in vocabulary. Then the teacher can provide suitable activities accordingly for each group of students. In that way, the students will be working on the specific language area that they most need to work on at that time.

Section II of the book consists of examples of grammatical structures frequently misused by Bronx Community College students when they did the activities. It can be used during and after the writing activity. If, while writing, some students have questions about structures they are using, or appear open to suggestions, they can be referred to the appropriate page to see if they can correct themselves by studying the examples. Or after they have finished writing and the teacher has indicated the errors, the students can be referred to the appropriate pages to help them correct their own work. This section can also be used before the students write if the teacher feels that the entire class needs guidance on a particular structure, for example, the use of direct or indirect speech in "An Unforgettable Night." When the section is used in this way it must be clear to the students that the teacher is giving them a tool to help them write more accurately because the writing requires it. In other words, the teaching is subordinate to the writing and not vice versa.

SEQUENCING

This book contains six types of activities:

1. Semicontrolled Writing
2. Story Completion
3. Model Composition
4. Dialogue Writing
5. Writing in response to a story
6. Writing in response to a picture

The selections have been sequenced according to the amount of reading involved, the length of the writing required by the activity and the amount of control built into the activity. For example, the semicontrolled writing selections, because of their greater control, come before the dialogues; moreover, within the semicontrolled selections, "The Super" comes before "The Fire" because "The Super" requires only three paragraphs and is more tightly controlled. However, the selections do not have to be used in order either according to categories or in order within categories. Generally speaking, the less advanced students will begin with the shorter, easier, more controlled activities, but sometimes even relatively good writers can benefit from some of the more controlled work. While the sequencing has been done according to the difficulty of each category viewed as a whole, individual activities within the first three categories may be easy enough for students to attempt at or near the beginning of a course. Selections from categories 4–6 and some from categories 1–3 become appropriate at that point in the course when students have indicated by their progress that they are ready for the longer, more difficult activities. Students in the high intermediate to low advanced range can conceivably begin almost anywhere in the book. Since the book is not intended to be used in any kind of strict order, teachers are responsible for knowing what activities the students are ready for.

OPTIONAL ACTIVITIES

The primary focus of this book is helping students to write better. The selections, because of their structure and value for students, lend themselves to other kinds of classroom activities, such as role playing, discussion, reading and retelling. Teachers should feel free to make these activities the primary focus of a lesson if they so wish. However, the authors see these activities as aiding the final writing process. Students, by investing themselves in the selections through role playing, retelling, etc., will have gained an understanding of the situation and a familiarity with some of the vocabulary which will aid them when they begin to write. Their initial investment in the optional activities can aid their further investment in the writing.

NOTES

1. Vocabulary lists are optional. If the teacher feels that the students can work well enough without the lists, they should be encouraged to do so.
2. Even though the activities already have titles, students should be encouraged to make up their own titles.
3. It has been the authors' experience that males for some reason have more difficulty playing a female role than females do playing a male role. With this is mind, optional activity No. 3 has been included in the dialogue "Luisa Rodriguez and Her Mother."

SEMICONTROLLED
WRITING

THE SUPER

ACTIVITY Write about your super. The questions below will help you. You may give additional information and examples.

1. Is the super an old or a young man? Does he have a family or is he single? Does he live in the basement or on one of the floors of the building? Does he speak English or some other language? Is he a friendly or an unfriendly person?

2. Does he keep the building clean or does he let it get dirty? Does he keep children out of the lobby or does he allow them to play there? In winter does he provide enough heat or does he keep the boiler shut off? When something is broken, does he fix it himself or does he call a repairman? Does he put the garbage out on time or does he let it pile up in the basement?

3. Do the tenants like the super or not? What do they give him at Christmas time?

OPTIONAL ACTIVITIES

1. Working in pairs Write this story with a partner. You and your partner decide together what details you want to include in your story. Both of you write exactly the same thing on your papers. When you have finished, check each other's papers to make sure you have written the same thing and have spelled all the words correctly.

2. Interview Ask your partner to tell you about his or her super. Then you tell your partner about your super.

HARRY

ACTIVITY   Write about Harry. Use the following questions as a guide.

1.   What nationality is Harry? Is he married or single? Does he have children? Where does he live? How many rooms does his apartment have? How much rent does he pay? Does he live in a nice neighborhood? Are his neighbors sociable? Do they talk with Harry when they see him?

2.   Where does Harry work? What does he do? How many days a week does he work? How much money does he make a week? Is he satisfied with his job? Does he have a chance for a promotion? Do his coworkers like him?

3.   What does he like to do on weekends? Does he go out alone or with his wife or with his girl friend? Do friends come to his home for a visit? Does he like to stay up late on Sunday nights?

OPTIONAL ACTIVITY

Working in pairs   Write this story with a partner. You and your partner decide together what details you want to include in your story. Both of you write exactly the same thing on your papers. When you have finished, check each other's papers to make sure you have written the same thing and have spelled all the words correctly.

MARIE STAMMATI

ACTIVITY   Write about Marie Stammati. Use the following questions as a guide.

1. Her early life:
   Born: in Naples, Italy; May 14, 1958.
   Parents: poor. Her father: a baker. Her mother: a housewife with _____ children.
   Neighborhood: clean or dirty? Where did she play? Who did she play with?
   Elementary school: What kind of school did she go to? Her teachers: good or bad? Her classmates: from the same economic class? What were her favorite subjects?
2. Her teenage years:
   High School: entered as a freshman, September 1972. What was her major subject? Why?
   Problems: mother died in 1973. What did Marie's father ask her? What did Marie decide to do? Was she happy or unhappy with her decision? Why?
   Good luck: What happened to Marie when she was nineteen?

OPTIONAL ACTIVITY
Working in pairs   Write this story with a partner. You and your partner decide together what details you want to include in your story. Both of you write exactly the same thing on your papers. When you have finished, check each other's papers to make sure that you have written the same thing and have spelled all the words correctly.

THE FORTUNE TELLER

You are at a party and an interesting looking person comes up to you and offers to tell your future by "reading your palm." You agree to it. The fortune teller looks closely at your hand for a minute and then tells you what will happen in your life in the future.

ACTIVITY Write out the words of the fortune teller predicting what will happen to you in your life. Begin this way:

The fortune teller said: I will . . .

The following are suggestions for questions the fortune teller might answer:

1. How long will you live? Will you be healthy or ill most of your life?

2. Will you marry? (If you are already married, how long will you stay married?) Will you have children? (If you already have children, will you have more?) Will you have grandchildren? How many? Boys or girls? Will you be happy with your family life?

Or

Will you stay single? Will you live alone or with other people? Will you be happy being single?

3. How far will you go with your education? What will you study? Will you get a degree? What kind? In what field of study? Will you learn English well? What will you be able to do in English that you can't do now?

4. What kind of work will you do? Will you change jobs often? Will you have your own business or go into a profession? Will you make much money? Will you be happy with your work?

5. Where will you spend most of your life? In this country? Which part? Or, back in your native country? Or, in some other country?

6. Will you travel? To which countries? Why? With whom?

7. Will there be any disappointments in your life? Are there things that you want to do that you will not be able to? Are there things that you want to have that you will not be able to?

8. What will be the happiest and/or the most satisfying part of your life? Will people remember you after you are gone? Who? Why?

Helpful words and phrases

You will find many helpful words in the selection above. Here are some more words and phrases that our students used when they wrote this story:

happy	lucky	always
happily	trouble	often
happiness	family	until
health	parents	
healthy	business	
kindness	neighborhood	

Words that our students sometimes confuse:

live — life	where — were	quite — quiet
when — went	too much — very much	believe — belief

Expressions:

when you are able	all of your children
the reason that	a couple of your children
your whole life	one of the best _____s

OPTIONAL ACTIVITY

Tell what the fortune teller said in reported (indirect) speech. Begin this way:

   The fortune teller said that I would _____

A LETTER HOME

ACTIVITY   Write a letter to a friend or relative telling about yourself. Use the following questions as a guide.

1. Ask your correspondent how he/she is feeling. Tell him/her how you are feeling.

2.   What are you doing right now (in addition to writing this letter)? Are you eating or drinking anything as you are writing this letter? What are the other people in your home or class doing right now? Is anything happening outside or in the room at this moment?

3. Where are you living now? Whom are you living with? Are you working? Where? What kind of work are you doing? Are you going to school this year? Where? What are you studying? What courses are you taking this semester?

4. What are you doing after class or this evening? Where are you having dinner tonight or tomorrow night? What are you having? Are you having anyone over for dinner this week? What are you serving?

5. Are you buying or getting something new soon (clothing, a television set, a stereo, a car, a new apartment or home)? Are you starting to do anything new? What? When? What are you planning to do in the future?

6. Ask your correspondent to write to you soon.

YOUR LETTER SHOULD LOOK LIKE THIS:

Your Address
Today's Date

Dear _____,

How are you feeling? I _____

_____.

_____

_____

_____ .

Yours truly,
(Sign your name)

(You may also close a friendly letter with *Sincerely,/Your friend,/With love,/Affectionately,/All my love,/Love,*)

THE FIRE

Recently there was a fire in your neighborhood. You and your friend watched the fire and saw everything that happened.

ACTIVITY Write about what you saw. You may use any details you wish in your writing. The following questions can guide you in your selection and organization of details.

1. Where was the fire: In your building? Across the street? At the end of the block? In a store? In a vacant building? In your best friend's apartment? When did the fire occur? At what time did the fire start? Where were you when the fire started?

2. What was the fire caused by: A child playing with matches? A faulty electrical circuit? Food left to burn on the stove? Was the fire accidental? Was it set by an arsonist?

3. Who reported the fire? How did this person report the fire: By phone? By pulling the alarm at the corner? By running to the fire house? By stopping a passing patrol car? How many engines and firemen responded to the alarm? How long did it take for the fire engines to arrive at the fire? What did you and your friend do when you heard the engines coming onto your block?

4. What did the firemen do when they first arrived? Did they locate the fire right away? Was the fire serious? What did they do to put out the fire? Did they use: fire hoses? ladders? axes? Did they have to rescue someone trapped inside the building?

5. How long did it take them to put out the fire? How much damage did the fire do: The entire building? Only one floor? Only one apartment? Did the fire spread to other buildings and damage them also? Were any people injured? Were any firemen injured? Were any families left homeless?

6. What did you and your friend do after the firemen left?

Helpful words and phrases

You will find many helpful words in the selection above. Here are some more words and phrases that our students used when they wrote this story:

Words		*Phrases*
destroyed	broke out	was caused by
hurt	put out	were damaged
immediately	last night	were left homeless
insurance	as soon as	was destroyed
landlord	when	was burned
neighbor	after	was ruined
rescue	broke	went out of
responsible	broken	spread to
situation	called	had been living
smoke	occurred	took a long time
tenants	screamed	to see where the fire was
too	stopped	one of the firemen
whole	told	a friend of ours
		in a building
		into the street
		a neighbor's building

OPTIONAL ACTIVITY

Working in pairs Write this story with a partner. You and your partner decide together what details you want to include in your story. Both of you write exactly the same thing on your papers. When you have finished, check each other's papers to make sure you have written the same thing and have spelled all the words correctly.

THE ROBBERY

ACTIVITY   Write about a robbery which occurred recently. You may use any details you wish in writing your story. The following questions can guide you in your selection and organization of details.

NOTE   The word *employee* has been written with an (s) after it to indicate that you may choose to write about only one employee, for example, a storekeeper, or you may choose to write about several employees, for example, bank tellers.

1.   Where was the robbery? In a small grocery store? In a bank? In a large clothing store? What is the name of the place that was robbed? Where is it located? When did the robbery occur? At what time did the robbery occur?
2.   How many robbers were there? What sex were they? Were they old or young? Tall or short? What were they wearing? What kind of weapons, if any, did they carry?
3.   What did the robbers tell the employee(s) to do? What did the robbers take? Money? Jewels? Clothing? Nothing? What did the robbers do to the employee(s) before they left? Was anyone injured?
4.   What did the employee(s) do after the robbers left? Did the police come? What did the police do? Chase the robbers? Question the employee(s)? Nothing? Were the robbers caught?
5.   How do the employee(s) feel about the robbery? Calm? Angry? Afraid? What will the employee(s) do in the future? Carry a gun? Get a job in a safer neighborhood? Move out of the city? Keep a watchdog in the place?

Helpful words and phrases

You will find many helpful words in this selection. Here are some more words and phrases that our students used when they wrote this story.

answer	all the money	keep quiet
cashier	blow up	took place
customer	couldn't do anything	was/were scared
teller	got loose	shot
thief	"Hands up!"	stolen
thieves	no one was	
threaten	someone was	

Infinitive and past tense forms of some verbs used by our students:

to catch	— caught	to start	— started
to chase	— chased	to steal	— stole
to drive	— drove	to take	— took
to identify	— identified	to tell	— told
to leave	— left	to tie (up)	— tied (up)
to occur	— occurred	to watch	— watched
to rob	— robbed	to wear	— wore
to shoot	— shot		

OPTIONAL ACTIVITY

Working in pairs Write this story with a partner. You and your partner decide together what details you want to include in your story. Both of you write exactly the same thing on your papers. When you have finished, check each other's papers to make sure you have written the same thing and have spelled all the words correctly.

THE WEDDING

ACTIVITY Next week David Bloomfield and Maria Redfern are getting married. You are close friends with one or both of them. Write about them, their wedding and their plans. You may use any of the details below that you wish or you may add your own details.

NOTE In writing this story you will have to use several verb tenses. The wedding will take place in the *future*, but you will have to use the *past* and *present* in parts of the story, for example, when you describe the bride and groom.

1. The wedding: Time? Place? Will it be a church wedding or a civil ceremony? Who and how many will be in the bridal party? Dress? Reception? Number of guests?

2. Description of the bride: Physical appearance? Age? Much older or younger than the groom? Who is she? Married before? Career woman? Sewing machine operator? Reason for wanting to get married: Love? Money? Desire to escape from her parents? Looking for a substitute father?

3. Description of the groom: Physical appearance? Age? Much older or younger than the bride? Who is he? Married before? Widower with five kids? Factory worker? Prosperous doctor? Reason for wanting to get married: Love? Money? Desire to escape from his parents? Looking for a substitute mother?

4. Reaction of the bride's parents to the wedding: Happy? Upset with the idea of losing their daughter? Like the groom? Why? Dislike the groom? Why? Threatened to do something if their daughter marries him? What? Cut her off from the family inheritance? Refuse to see her again? Told the groom to leave the country and not marry their daughter?

5. Plans: Honeymoon? Where? How long? Where will they live? In a luxurious apartment on Park Avenue? In a tenement in the South Bronx? With the bride's parents? Planning to raise a family?

Helpful words and phrases
You will find many helpful words in this selection. Here are some more words and phrases that our students used when they wrote this story.

afford	guests	minister
beautiful	happiness	neighborhood
daughter	judge	priest
future	lawyer	secretary

at the wedding
planning to get married
in love
love each other
She is 20 (twenty).
She is 20 years old.
He is 21 (twenty-one).

OPTIONAL ACTIVITY
Working in pairs   Write this story with a partner. You and your partner decide together what details you want to include in your story. Both of you write exactly the same thing on your papers. When you have finished, check each other's papers to make sure you have written the same thing and have spelled all the words correctly.

A LECTURE

ACTIVITY Pretend that you return to your native country after spending some time in the United States and are asked to lecture to a group of university students about life in the United States. Write out in English the lecture that you will give. When you prepare the lecture, think about the kinds of questions university students in your country might ask and try to answer them. For example, in the parts of the United States you have lived in or visited:

1. Are most Americans friendly to foreigners? Do they usually try to help? Are they courteous in stores and on trains and busses? Do they try to understand if you have difficulty with English? Is it easy to make friends with Americans?

2. Are most Americans rich? Do they all have big cars? Do most of them have refrigerators, washing machines, dishwashers, color television? Are most of them generous?

3. How do most students dress? What kind of clothing do they wear? What do they wear to parties, to weddings, to school?

4. Is it easy to get a job in the United States? What kinds of jobs can you get if you don't speak much English?

5. Is it easy to get into school? Is it expensive? How is school in the United States different from school in your native country? Do the teachers treat you differently? Is the work easier or more difficult? Is it difficult if you don't know much English? Can you learn English in school?

6. Is there much crime in the United States? What kind? Do many Americans have guns? Is life in America the same as shown on television and in films?

7. How are women treated? Can they get good jobs? Can they go out alone to parties, to bars, to the movies?

8. When do most Americans eat meals? Which foods and beverages do many of them like? Where do some of them go on weekends? What kind of entertainment do they like?

9. Are there any other questions that someone might ask you? Is there anything else important that you should tell about the United States?

OPTIONAL ACTIVITIES

1. Compare your answers to some of the questions above with another student or a group of students in the class before you write your lecture.

2. Write about one aspect of American life such as the rights of women, comparing it to the situation in your country.

STORY
COMPLETION

THE LOTTERY

I sat there with two other people—all of us finalists—waiting for them to draw the lucky name. One of us would win the lottery and one million dollars. The Governor reached into the bowl and drew out a piece of paper. He slowly unfolded it and then paused to look at the audience. He smiled at the television and movie cameras. I wanted to scream "Hurry up!" Finally, he looked at the paper and read the name. IT WAS MINE!

ACTIVITY Complete this story telling what happened after you won the lottery.

Helpful words and phrases
Here are some words and phrases that our students used when they completed this story.

all of a sudden	a six-month trip
put down a deposit	everything was O.K./okay
$1000 worth of _____	at the time

accept	exhausted	nervous
comfortable	explain	money
congratulations	future	prize
deposit	interview	responsible
donated	lucky	shocked
especially	neighborhood	truth

Here are the infinitive and past tense forms of some verbs our students used in writing this story:

to wake	— waked, woke	to buy	— bought
to awake	— awaked, awoke	to find	— found
to leave	— left	to help	— helped
to let	— let	to hug	— hugged
to lose	— lost	to meet	— met
to lie	— lay	to offer	— offered
to listen	— listened	to put	— put
to reply	— replied	to spend	— spent
to cry	— cried	to send	— sent
to pray	— prayed	to think	— thought
to pay	— paid	to throw	— threw
to fall	— fell	to watch	— watched
to feel	— felt	to win	— won

OPTIONAL ACTIVITIES

1. Pretend you are being interviewed by a newspaper reporter. Tell the reporter what you plan to do with the money.

2. Pretend it is now six months after you won the money. Write a letter to a friend telling him or her what you are doing right now.

THE CAVE

Last Sunday Tom and Ellen went on a picnic. They were lovers and were expecting to spend a pleasant day together. But in the middle of the afternoon it started to rain. They looked around for a place to get out of the rain. Nearby they saw a cave.

ACTIVITY   Finish the story.

Helpful words and phrases
Here are some words and phrases that our students used when they completed this story.

afraid	a few minutes later
alone	all day
disappointed	in the meantime
heavily	on their way
pleasant	the whole night
sandwiches	too late
silent	wet from the rain
decided to ask	The rain stopped
lit a match	It stopped raining
made/built a fire	The day turned out ...
needed one another	It scared them
suggested that they walk	It made them scared
told each other	

Infinitives and past tense forms of some verbs used by our students:

to ask	— asked	to put	— put
to bring	— brought	to reply	— replied
to grab	— grabbed	to run	— ran
to lie (down)	— lay (down)	to ruin	— ruined
to listen	— listened	to stand	— stood

to stay	— stayed
to stop	— stopped
to think	— thought
to yell	— yelled

ON THE BEACH

It was getting dark. Tony and Alice were lying together on the beach. Except for them the beach was deserted. Everything was quiet and peaceful except for the sound of the sea.

Suddenly, they saw something moving in the water near them.

ACTIVITY Finish the story.

OUT OF GAS

Bill Richardson, an American, was on vacation in this beautiful country. He was driving alone along a narrow mountain road trying to get to Canstaadt, a lovely mountain village. It was 9:00 at night, very dark and cold, and Bill was getting scared. He knew that it was dangerous in the mountains especially at night. Several people had disappeared in these mountains during the past couple of weeks and no one could find them. At that moment the car slowed down and then stopped. Bill looked at the fuel gauge. "Oh, no!" he groaned, "The car is out of gas." He got out of the car and looked around. He couldn't see anyone or anything. He sat down at the side of the road to think.

Suddenly, he heard a noise.

ACTIVITY Finish the story.

AN UNFORGETTABLE NIGHT

The night started out so well for us. Bill picked me up on time and we were off to a night of dancing at the Casa Blanca. We had been looking forward to this night for two weeks, ever since we heard that Johnny Ventura and his Orchestra were going to play.

Bill parked around the corner from the club and we went in. We were early on purpose so that we could get a table near the dance floor and the orchestra. A waiter brought us a bottle of White Label and we sat sipping our drinks. Gradually the club began to fill with other couples—women in bare-backed gowns or long-sleeved blouses and flowing, calf length skirts; men in jacket and tie or wide collar shirts and vests. Everyone looked beautiful. They sat or stood in groups talking excitedly while waiting for their favorite orchestra to appear.

Finally Johnny and his group arrived. They quickly set up on the stage, warmed up, and were ready to play. As they began their first number—a merengue, of course—Bill and I jumped up to dance. We were happy in each other's arms, dancing to the swirling rhythms of the orchestra. We didn't sit down again until they had finished the first set. While they took a break, Bill and I sat talking about our plans. We had become engaged a month before and were planning to get married in June. We had some problems to iron out, but we were confident that we could solve them. We were happy knowing that we loved each other and would soon be starting our life together.

The music started again and we danced the second set. While the orchestra took another break, I went to the ladies room. It took a few minutes because the room was crowded. When I left the ladies room, I saw someone else at our table. Bill was sitting where I had left him, but a girl I had never seen before was standing next to him. She was leaning over him, and her long shiny black hair was brushing against his cheek. He was holding her hand and his eyes looked into hers. Suddenly she leaned over even further and kissed him. He didn't pull his lips away.

I stood still for a moment, watching them. Then slowly I walked over to the table.

ACTIVITY   Finish the story.

OPTIONAL ACTIVITIES

1.   Write about what you would have done if you had been the woman in this situation. Begin this way:

If I had been the woman I would have . . .

2.   Pretend that you are Bill and finish the story.

BOB

Bob liked Barcelona. He frequently walked up and down the Ramblas looking at the people. He often stopped to browse at the magazine stands or to watch the vendors selling handicrafts and lottery tickets and birds and rabbits. Then he liked to sit down at one of the cafes, have a drink, and watch the people again. Some evenings he wandered through the old part of the city stopping in small, noisy bars for a glass of wine and some snacks they called *tapas*, like the sausage called *chorizo* which they covered in a clear, flavored brandy and set on fire— *al diablo*—before eating.

Although he didn't speak Spanish, within a month Bob felt very much at home. He met a lot of English-speaking people who were friendly and helpful. One helped him find a job, another an apartment. He learned enough Spanish words so that he could get the things he needed in shops and order what he wanted in restaurants. But most of the time, the only language he needed was English. He spoke to his friends in English. He read English newspapers and heard broadcasts from England on his short-wave radio to find out what was happening in the world. He even found some English-language films to see. And on his job teaching English to bank clerks every morning, he didn't have to speak the language of his students. Most of the time he didn't try. It was certainly much easier to speak your own language than to speak another one, letting people know that you were a foreigner and taking the risk of having them laugh at you.

But there was a lot missing. He couldn't understand television or go to the theater, and he felt isolated from the things that were going on in this city and country he was living in. He also knew that he could not get a good full-time job and make enough money to live comfortably without being able to speak and read and write Spanish very well. He knew that it would be difficult to do, but if he didn't try, he would have to go back to the United States, where he had no job, no family, and few friends. And he didn't want to do that.

ACTIVITY   A.   Read and think about the following questions:

  1.   What two choices did Bob have?
  2.   What did he want to do? Why?
  3.   Why did he prefer life in Barcelona to life in a big city in the United States?
  4.   Why was it difficult for him to learn Spanish?
  5.   What did he have to do (and what did he have to *stop* doing) if he wanted to learn Spanish well?
  6.   Try to describe Bob. How old was he? What kind of education did he have? What did he enjoy doing?
  7.   What decision do you think he made?

B.   Now complete Bob's story. Tell what Bob did and how he did it. Be specific—give details.

Helpful words and phrases

You will find many helpful words in this story. Here are some more words and phrases that our students used when they wrote this story.

always	passers-by	more/less expensive
language	profession	(much) cheaper
necessary	really	got in touch with
		moved in with

Here are the infinitive and past tense forms of some verbs our students used in writing this story:

to feel	— felt	to start	— started
to hear	— heard	to begin	— began
to say	— said	to stop	— stopped
to speak	— spoke	to stay	— stayed
to laugh	— laughed	to stand	— stood
to read	— read	to sit	— sat
to study	— studied	to make	— made
to enroll	— enrolled	to plan	— planned
		to buy	— bought

OPTIONAL ACTIVITIES

1. Retelling. Tell Bob's story to a partner or other members of the class.

2. Working in pairs. With a partner, answer the questions at the end of the story.

MODEL
COMPOSITIONS

AN INTERVIEW WITH HOSSEIN

My classmate's name is Hossein Hassad. He comes from the Middle East. He has been in this country for only one year. He is single but he has a steady girl friend. He lives with his aunt and uncle. His parents and brothers and sisters are in Iran. He came to this country to finish his education. He's studying to be an electrical engineer.

Hossein has many interests besides school. He enjoys disco music and he often takes his girl friend dancing. He also likes photography. He showed me some pictures that he took. They were excellent.

Hossein says that he likes this school and he likes this country, but he plans to go back to his native country after he graduates.

ACTIVITY   Interview a classmate and then write a short composition about him or her.

Ask your classmate questions such as, "Where are you from?" "Who do you live with?". Write down the answers.

Then use the information to write a composition about your classmate. You may use the composition about Hossein as a model.

OPTIONAL ACTIVITY

Tell the class about the person you interviewed before you write about him or her.

A FAVORITE DISH

My father grew up in Romania, and one of his special memories was of the eggplant salad that his mother used to prepare. My father used to make it in our home, but he said it never tasted quite the same as it did when his mother made it. She used to take a freshly picked eggplant and cook it on top of a woodburning stove until it was slightly burned on the outside and soft on the inside. My father said his mouth used to water when he smelled the burnt aroma of that lovely fresh eggplant, and that he could hardly wait for dinner time to taste the sharp smokey flavor. My father made it for us only on holidays, cooking the eggplant on top of our gas stove, and I can remember when I was a child looking forward to tasting that delicious dish, just as my father had when he was a child.

Papa Marco's Eggplant Salad

Select a firm eggplant, purple in color, weighing about 1 1/4 pounds. Wash it and put it directly on top of an oven burner over a very low flame. As it starts to burn, turn it so that every part of the vegetable is blackened and softened by the flame. This should take about 45 minutes. While the eggplant is cooking, chop one small onion into small pieces and saute it in oil in a frying pan until it is light brown. When the eggplant is done, remove it to a dish and let it cool. Then peel off the skin and put the vegetable into a bowl. Add two tablespoons of vegetable oil, one tablespoon of apple cider vinegar, 1/4 teaspoon of salt, a sprinkling of red pepper, and the sauteed onions. Mash the mixture with a fork until it is smooth. Serve on a large platter on a base of lettuce leaves. Garnish with sliced tomatoes, radishes, and green olives.

The soft, flat middle eastern bread called "pita" is excellent with this dish and can be used to scoop up the eggplant salad like a dip. I prefer to drink beer with this, but a chilled, very dry Greek or Romanian wine is a good accompaniment.

ACTIVITY   Think about one of the favorite dishes from your childhood. Try to remember all the ingredients that go into it and how it is prepared. Then write the recipe for the dish.

Helpful words and phrases
You will find many helpful words in this selection. Here are some more words and phrases that our students used when they wrote their own recipes.

teaspoon	add	stir	pot	mixing bowl
tablespoon	marinate	slice	pan	wok
ounce (oz.)	cook	chop	frying pan	casserole
pound (lb.)	boil	grate	stove	spatula
cup (=8 oz.)	fry	mince	oven	ladle
	mix	cut	bowl	
	blend	scramble	platter	

MY LIFE

I was born in Athens, Greece on January 11, 1957. My father was a businessman and my mother stayed home and took care of our house and family. I have four brothers and sisters; two sisters and a brother are older than I am and one brother is younger. When I was a child, my friends and I went everywhere we wanted, and my younger brother would tag along after me. We roamed the streets and climbed the hills, played soccer and gambled with cards or dice, and sometimes stole things from stores. My father used to punish me for doing some of these things.

From the ages of six to twelve I went to school in Athens, but I wasn't a very good student. In 1967 my family left Greece and came to this country. It was difficult for me at first because I didn't have any friends and I didn't understand the language, but I went to high school and made friends and learned a lot.

When I finished high school I went to work for my father. I also met a lovely Greek girl named Urania and we got married in June 1977. We have a one-year-old boy called Alexander. We live in a neighborhood where there are many Greek people and we keep many of the same customs we had in the old country. We eat many of the same foods and we practice the holidays in similar ways. I especially like the evening candle procession around the church at Easter.

Now that I have a family to take care of, I am much more serious about life than I used to be, and I have decided to return to school to get a degree in engineering and to improve my knowledge of the language. I would like to be an engineer some day.

ACTIVITY Think about the most important events and aspects of your life so far: for example, where and when you were born; your parents and brothers and sisters; your schooling; major moves; marriage; children. Also think about some specific incidents from your childhood or more recently that you might like to describe. Then, write about yourself.

Helpful words and phrases

You will find many helpful words and phrases in this story. Here are some more words and phrases that our students used in writing about themselves.

on June 11, 1970
in June
in 1970
I was born in (a country)
I got married
I married a man/woman named _____

I used to (infinitive form)
They didn't want me to _____
I tried to _____
in the eighth grade
in elementary school
in secondary school/high school

childhood
younger/older brother/sister
My parents moved to _____
We emigrated from _____
I am planning to

approximately
grateful
I had to (infinitive form)
a lot
impossible

THE BARBER SHOP

You have to climb a long flight of dimly lit stairs to get to Aida and Caroline's hair styling salon. But its big glass windows face out onto Broadway and the shop is light and pleasant. If you have an appointment, there is usually only a short wait.

First, Aida shampoos your hair. She puts a plastic covering over you and leans your head backward into a sink. She gives the hair two separate washes and then wraps a towel around your head to dry it. Next she seats you in the barber's chair and with scissors and comb spends almost an hour cutting your hair. There is a mirror in front of the chair with a shelf holding different kinds of hair dressings, each a different color and each in a different kind of bottle. The sinks and coat rack are in back of you and Caroline's chair is on the right. There are pictures of good-looking men with different hair styles around the mirror and on the wall to your left. As Aida cuts your hair she talks about herself and her family, and often about God. But you don't have to listen; she usually doesn't expect a response. If you have a beard, she will trim it for you before she's done. She is very careful and your hair always looks good when she's finished.

Aida likes having her shop on the second floor because it gives her customers privacy. In most barber shops you can look through the big glass windows and watch people getting their hair cut. Aida never liked that. She thinks a second floor shop has more "class." When she worked in another barber shop, friends would always come in to talk to her while she was cutting hair. That doesn't happen so much any more, but Aida thinks that's all right. After all, this isn't just a barber shop— it's a men's hair salon.

ACTIVITY Describe a barber shop or beauty parlor that you go to or are familiar with. You can write about:

the furniture and equipment
how it is decorated
what the customers are like
what the barbers or hair-
    dressers are like

how they cut or style hair
why you like (or don't like)
    to go there

Helpful words and phrases
You will find many helpful words and phrases in this story.
Here are some more words and phrases that our students used
in writing this description.

accessible	dryer	manicurist
attached	entrance	permanent
barber	haircut	placed
beautician	hairnet	pressed
blow dry	instructions	rollers
comfortable	manicure	setting
brushes	pours	satisfies
combs	puts	washes
finishes	rinses	
massages	rubs	

at the right
on the (other) side
one week in advance
in the process
pay attention to

ANECDOTE

Our professor of Comparative Religion seemed well suited to teach his subject. He looked like a biblical prophet with his ragged gray beard and serious face, and he always gave us difficult assignments.

It was not surprising then that on the day of our final examination we came into the classroom expecting the worst. As if reflecting our fears that day, the sky was dark and a storm threatened.

Right on time, the professor arrived and without even greeting us he began reading aloud his first question in a deep voice. Our fears had been justified. Not daring to make a sound, we could only wait quietly in our seats and listen to the endless question. It covered the entire semester's work, asking for detailed comparisons of the major religions and requiring specific information from the textbook and classroom notes.

He had barely finished reading when an angry sound of thunder came rumbling down from the overcast sky, ending in a tremendous roar that shook the room and rattled the windows. Without hesitating, our professor looked angrily upward, and shaking his finger at the ceiling overhead, thundered back, "And that's only the first question."

ACTIVITY Write about an amusing incident that you or someone you know experienced.

A LETTER OF COMPLAINT

888 West End Avenue
New York, N.Y. 10025
February 8, 19__

New York City Department of Consumer Affairs
80 Lafayette Street
New York, N.Y. 10001

Dear Sirs or Madams:

I would like to file a complaint against the Waverly Wines and Spirits Co., Inc. of 310 Waverly Place, Manhattan.

On October 15 of last year I telephoned an order for the following mechandise and mailed a check for $76.11 ($70.47 plus $5.64 sales tax).

1	1.75 liter bottle of Dawson Scotch @	$11.59
1	1.75 liter bottle of Ron Bacardi @	11.99
2	Fifths of Manischewitz Concord Wine @ 1.95	($3.90)
1	case of Marques de Murrieta red wine @	43.99

On November 4, after making several calls to the company, I finally received all of the merchandise except the case of Marques de Murrieta wine. An enclosed note said that the wine was out of stock and would be sent to me shortly.

When I had not received the wine by November 18, I called the company to cancel the order and asked for a refund of $47.51 ($43.99 plus $3.42 sales tax).

Since then I have called the company five or six times and written a letter (copy enclosed) but I have received neither the money nor the wine.

Before I spend the time and money to go to Small Claims Court, I would appreciate it if you would look into this matter for me. Copies of the original receipt and my cancelled check are enclosed.

Thank you for any help you can give me.

Yours truly,
David Davidson
David Davidson

cc: Waverly Wines and Spirits Co., Inc.

ACTIVITY Write a letter of complaint to an individual, a company or a government agency explaining in detail the situation you are unhappy about.

DIALOGUES

LUISA RODRIGUEZ
AND HER MOTHER

Mrs. Rodriguez came here from an island country in the Caribbean. Even though she's been here fifteen years, she still holds onto the ideas and customs of her native country. Her children follow the traditional custom of asking for her blessing whenever they leave the house. She doesn't allow her teenage daughter, Luisa, to go out alone. When Luisa comes home from school, she has to stay in the house. She isn't allowed to go to parties on the weekends or to go out with boys even though she's seventeen years old. Mrs. Rodriguez says she has to wait until she graduates from high school. She loves her daughter very much, but she is strict with her because she believes that is the best way to raise her children.

Luisa wasn't born here but she came here when she was a child. Since the third grade she's gone to American schools and has had American friends. Her friends stay outside on the street after school. They go to parties and on dates. Luisa wants to be with them and do what they do. Recently she became attracted to Tony, a boy in the same class at school. Tony has asked her to go out with him and she wants to accept. Luisa loves her mother and respects her ways, but she really would like her mother to give her more freedom. She knows that she's going to have a hard time convincing her mother.

Last night after her brothers and sisters had gone to bed, Luisa talked with her mother about Tony, her desire to go out with him and her desire to have more freedom like her friends have.

ACTIVITY In the form of a dialogue write the conversation that you think Luisa had with her mother. You and your partner will write this dialogue together. What do you think Luisa said to her mother last night? What did Mrs. Rodriguez say to her daughter? To help you decide what they said to each other remember that:

MRS. RODRIGUEZ
- loves her daughter.
- is raising her daughter in a traditional way.
- wants Luisa to wait until she graduates from high school before she starts going out with boys.

LUISA
- loves her mother.
- wants to be more like her American friends.
- likes Tony and wants to go out with him.

Write the dialogue like this:

LUISA: Mom, I want to talk you about something important.
MOTHER: O.K., Luisa, what is it?
LUISA: _____
MOTHER: _____

Remember that both you and your partner are responsible for sharing the ideas and the writing of this dialogue. Be sure to write both Luisa's sentences and her mother's sentences on one piece of paper so that the complete dialogue will be together. Also, be sure to give the dialogue a title.

Helpful words and phrases
You will find many helpful words in the story above. Here are some more words and phrases that our students used when they wrote this dialogue:

Words	*Phrases*
permit	give me a chance
permission	need your opinion
argument	change {your / my mind}
trouble	
understand	take care of {myself / yourself}
protect	
dangerous	treat like a child
disappoint	I was raised
obey	you were raised
disobey	I'm in love with

OPTIONAL ACTIVITIES

1. Retelling   After you have read about Mrs. Rodriguez and her daughter, tell the story again. Using your own words, explain what the story says about Luisa and her mother.

2. Role Playing   Before you do the writing activity, you and your partner play the roles of the two people in the story. One of you be Mrs. Rodriguez and one of you be Luisa. Have a conversation and say to each other the things you think Luisa and her mother would say to each other.

3.   Pretend that you are Luisa's older brother. You are responsible for her welfare because your mother had to return to her native country. With another member of the class, write out the conversation you and Luisa would have about this situation.

ANNA AND MARTIN

Anna and Martin are married and have been living in the United States for ten years. Martin drives a delivery truck and earns enough money to pay the rent on their four room apartment and to buy enough food and clothing for them and their two young children, a boy and a girl. But he also likes to go out a couple of nights a week to drink and play cards, or to go to a ball game with his friends. Anna doesn't mind his going out, but there is no money left over for her to do the things she would like to do. She would also like to save some money to buy a house and some special things for the children. She has decided that she would like to go to work.

She hasn't discussed this with Martin yet, but she thinks he would not approve. First of all, in their native country it is not as common for women to work as it is in the United States. Secondly, she knows that Martin is very proud and would not like the idea of his wife working. He thinks a wife should stay home and take care of her own home and family. She thinks there are enough good reasons for her to go to work, and she decides to discuss the situation with Martin. One night, after the children are asleep, she brings up the matter.

ACTIVITY In the form of a dialogue write the conversation that you think Anna had with Martin.

You and your partner will write this dialogue together. What do you think Anna said to her husband? What did Martin say to his wife? To help you decide what they said to each other remember that:

ANNA
{
loves and respects her husband and was brought up to think that "a woman's place is in the home," but they need the money, and besides, this is modern America and many women work.

would like money of her own to spend as she pleases without having to ask for it or to give explanations.

doesn't have enough to keep her occupied all day long; she gets bored.

feels there is something unfair about the marriage.
}

MARTIN
{
wouldn't like the idea of his wife contributing to support the family and having money of her own to spend any way she wants.

came to America to have a better life, not so his wife would have to work.

likes to know that his children are taken care of when they get home from school.
}

Write the dialogue like this:

ANNA: _____

MARTIN: _____

Remember that both you and your partner are responsible for sharing the ideas and the writing of this dialogue.

Be sure to write both Anna's sentences and Martin's sentences on one piece of paper so that the complete dialogue will be together.

Also, be sure to give the dialogue a title.

Helpful words and phrases

You will find many helpful words in the story above. Here are some more words and phrases that our students used when they wrote this dialogue:

Words	Phrases
earn	we have lots of expenses
independent	the children will grow up educated and healthy
salary	the head of this household
gambling	I can't convince you
income	change {my mind / your mind}
promise	
save	
complain	
support	

OPTIONAL ACTIVITIES

1. Retelling After you have read about Anna and her husband, Martin, tell the story again. Using your own words, explain what the story says about them.

2. Role Playing Before you do the writing activity, you and your partner play the roles of the two people in the story. One of you be Anna and one of you be Martin. Have a conversation and say to each other the things you think Anna and Martin would say to each other.

TERRY HARRIS
AND HIS FATHER

Mr. Harris, a wealthy, well-known lawyer, is paying for his son's education. He has plans for his son, Terry. He wants him to become a successful lawyer like himself. He dreams that Terry will be a partner in his law firm, will live in a mansion in an exclusive suburb, and will marry a beautiful, educated woman from a "good family."

Twenty-year-old Terry has other ideas. He's sick of college. He has decided that a career in law is just not for him. He wants to drop out of college at the end of the semester. Terry is also in love with Nancy, a waitress who works in a coffee shop near the campus. He wants to marry her.

Terry went home last weekend to talk to his father about his plans.

ACTIVITY Write in the form of a dialogue the conversation that you think took place between Terry and his father.

Helpful words and phrases
You will find some helpful words and phrases in this story. Here are some more words and phrases that our students used in writing this dialogue.

approve	an important thing
curriculum	important things
intellectual	to dream — dreamed, dreamt
ridiculous	
successful	

OPTIONAL ACTIVITIES

1. Retelling Explain to a partner or a group of students the conflict between Terry and his father.

2. Role Playing With a partner, play the roles of Terry Harris and his father. Act out the conversation they might have in this situation.

JOSE AND ANA

Jose and Ana are married. They have been living in New York for five years. They came to New York together from their native country, _____ , where they were married twelve years ago. They have two children, Leo, who is ten years old, and Sara, who is four.

Ana wants to go back to _____ , but Jose does not. Ana says it would be better for the children. They would have nicer friends, not get into trouble, and have a better education. There is less crime in _____ , the weather is more pleasant, and it is cheaper and easier to live there.

Jose says that he can earn a much better living in New York. All his friends are here now. The children will be better off because they will be able to get a free college education and eventually get good jobs. He calls the United States "the land of opportunity."

One evening, Jose and Ana discuss this matter.

ACTIVITY   Write in the form of a dialogue the conversation that you think took place between Jose and Ana.

JOHN AND CYNTHIA BARTON

John is fed up. He can't take any more of it. Nora, his mother-in-law, has got to go! When his wife, Cynthia, first suggested that her mother come to live with them for a while, John thought it was a good idea. But now that she's been living in his house for five months? Forget it! John wishes his mother-in-law would go to the moon. She's too nosy. She has to know everything that's going on. When he and Cynthia have a disagreement over something, the mother-in-law has to butt in with her opinion. It's impossible to have any privacy. She's costing John money, too. She makes frequent calls to friends back in Chicago and talks with them for hours. His monthly phone bills are enormous. And if all this wasn't enough, John knows that Nora doesn't like him. She feels her daughter could've found a better husband. Because of all this, John wants his mother-in-law out.

Cynthia is glad that her mother's living with them. Nora is a big help with the children. Cynthia leaves the children with her when she has to go out. The children like their grandma because she always has candy or cookies for them. Cynthia also appreciates her company. Sometimes John works over-time and gets home late. On those nights Cynthia doesn't have to wait up alone. Nora also helps with the housework and the cooking. Cynthia's life would be much more difficult if her mother wasn't there.

Tonight when John comes from work, he's going to talk to Cynthia about his mother-in-law.

ACTIVITY   In the form of a dialogue write the conversation you think John and Cynthia will have tonight.

STEVE AND ELIZABETH

Elizabeth has been going with Steve for almost a year and the relationship has become serious. She has the feeling that Steve's about to ask her to marry him. Elizabeth feels she's not ready to get married. She's in her second year of college and she wants to finish college and begin her career before she thinks about marriage and a family. Besides, she's only nineteen and Steve's her first real boy friend. Even though she's in love with him, she's not sure he's the man she wants to spend the rest of her life with.

Steve is twenty-six. He's very much in love with Elizabeth. He's had other girl friends. Now, after going out with Elizabeth for a year, he knows he's found the right woman to be his wife and the mother of his children. Nothing short of marriage will do for him. He's crazy about her and wants to be married to her for the rest of his life.

While out on a very special date Saturday night, Steve plans to propose to Elizabeth.

ACTIVITY In the form of a dialogue, write the conversation that you think Elizabeth and Steve will have when he asks her to marry him.

READ AND WRITE

AIDA

Aida calls herself a "hair stylist." She cuts and styles men's hair in a "salon" on the second floor of a building on Broadway. She and her friend Caroline used to work together in another barber shop on Broadway, but they recently decided to open their own business.

Aida is about fifty years old and is an attractive woman. She came from Cuba fifteen years ago and speaks English with some difficulty and with a heavy accent. She prefers to speak Spanish. Caroline, who is young and who went to school in the United States, conducts most of the business with salesmen and the landlord.

Aida has two grown children, a son and a daughter. The son married when he was nineteen and now has a child of his own. He was in the army for three years, but now he is a civilian without a good profession or skill. Aida helps them as much as she can. She particularly likes her daughter-in-law, who was "just a baby" when she married. Aida's own daughter is twenty years old and is in her second year of college. Aida wants her to finish school before getting married. "Don't ruin your life like your brother did," she cautions.

Aida's family was well-off in Cuba. Her parents died when she was young and she was raised by her paternal grandparents. Her grandfather was a successful businessman who had been born in Cuba. But her grandmother came from Spain and thought she was "special." And she raised Aida to think that she was "special" too. Aida received a good education "for a girl" in those days (she finished high school), and she was raised to have absolute faith in God. She has a small sign on the wall near her barber's chair which reads, *Sin Dios, Nada; Con Dios, Todo.*

Aida's husband was a businessman like her grandfather, and when he came to the United States for better opportunities, she came with him, bringing her two small children. Her husband died and she had to support herself and her family, so she learned how to be a hair stylist.

Aida has a lot of customers, mostly businessmen, and you usually need an appointment to see her in the late afternoon or on Saturday. She is an excellent hair stylist.

ACTIVITY Write about a person who came from another country to the United States as an adult.

Did he/she have to learn a new skill or profession? Describe it.

Did he/she have a family to take care of? A spouse? Children? Parents? Tell what happened.

How did the person learn English? In school? From reading? From friends? On the job? From television? Explain. How successful was he/she in learning English?

In what ways did he/she have to adjust to life in the United States?

Is this person happy and leading a satisfying life? Would he/she prefer to go back to his/her native country? Explain your answers and give specific examples: things that he/she does and says.

THE GROCERY STORE

Charlie owns a small grocery store on the corner of Longwood Avenue and Fox Street. Charlie is a nice guy. All the people in the neighborhood know he is a nice guy. Charlie's store is a little-of-everything-for-everybody kind of store. It carries all kinds of groceries, fresh and canned. It has meat, eggs and cheese. For the kids there are potato chips, candy and soda. In the back of the store there is a shelf for school supplies, novelties and coloring books. Behind the counter Charlie keeps cigarettes, aspirin, band-aids and other useful items. Charlie also has a machine to slice meat and cheese for sandwiches.

People run in and out of the store all day long and half way into the night. Sometimes one person will come in five or six times the same day. Usually it is a little girl who is sent by her mother to buy milk for the baby or more rice for supper or some bananas. Charlie doesn't mind all the business, of course, but

69

if the mother has credit at the store, he has a lot of extra bookkeeping to do.

Charlie opens his store early in the morning. He makes sure that the shelves are filled and then goes outside and carefully sweeps the sidewalk in front. He doesn't want to get a summons from the police. One of his first customers is Mr. Randall. He comes in every morning on his way to work to buy a pack of king-size Marlboro. Mr. Randall is cheerful in the morning. He has a good-paying job and he is proud of it.

A little while later some neighborhood kids come in with quarters to get some breakfast. They usually buy potato chips or soda. Charlie thinks to himself, "No wonder they are so skinny!" When the kids leave for school it is quiet for a while. Then the women begin to come in to get their groceries for the day. They aren't in any hurry. They stand around and talk about what is going on in their building. Charlie turns off his ears to the gossip. One of the women, Carolyn Maxwell, doesn't listen to the gossip, either. She prefers to talk to Charlie. Charlie thinks that she likes him a lot, but he doesn't want to get involved. She has four kids.

And so the day goes by. When school lets out, the kids play in the street. They run in with dimes and nickels clutched in their sweaty hands. They want soda. Teenage girls look through love stories before deciding which one to buy. Finally Phillip arrives to help him. Phillip is always late but he always has an excuse ready for Charlie. Some of them make Charlie laugh.

Charlie leaves Phillip in charge and goes out to get some supper and a couple of hours rest. At 7:30 he is back. The men are outside now. One or two are fixing their cars. A group is standing on the corner drinking beer and telling jokes. This is the dangerous time of day. It is always possible that someone may start a fight and break his store window. Or maybe someone will try to rob him.

Charlie does a lot of business at night, but he is glad when 11:30 comes and it is time to close up. He shuts the gate, locks it and goes home exhausted. Early tomorrow morning he will be back to take his place again in the life of the people of Longwood Avenue at the corner of Fox Street.

ACTIVITY   Write about a storekeeper or clerk who works in a small store in your neighborhood, or one that you go to frequently in another part of your city or town.

OPTIONAL ACTIVITIES

1.   Questions for Comprehension   Either by yourself or with a partner answer the following questions to help you understand the story better.

> What does Charlie do each day when he opens the store?
> Who comes to Charlie's store in the morning? In the afternoon? At night?
> Why does Charlie leave Phillip in charge of the store in the late afternoon?
> How does Charlie feel about keeping his store open at night? What does he worry about?
> When it is time to close the store, what does Charlie do? How does he feel?
> How do Charlie's customers feel about him?
> How does Charlie feel about his customers?
> How does Charlie help the neighborhood where his store is located?

2.   Retelling   After you have read about Charlie, tell the story again. Using your own words explain what the story says about Charlie and his store.

UNCLE CARMINE

I remember my Uncle Carmine. He used to come to my house almost every weekend during the fall and winter months of the hunting season. My uncle loved to hunt. He lived in a big city. We lived in the country. He used to keep his 12-gauge shotgun, ammunition and hunting jacket in a special closet in our basement. He used to arrive early Saturday morning, walking up the hill from the train station carrying two large round loaves of Italian bread wrapped in brown paper and tied together with a string. I always looked forward to his visits because I loved to eat that bread, but especially because Uncle Carmine always took me hunting with him. I loved to walk by his side always keeping slightly behind him. He insisted on this in case he had to raise his gun to his shoulder quickly and fire. We used to hunt rabbits. When he shot one, he brought it home, skinned it and let it soak in vinegar until it was ready to be made into rabbit stew. That rabbit stew was delicious. My mother cooked it for us. It tasted especially good to me because I knew that I had helped bring it to the table.

We used to begin the hunt in the woods behind my house. Soon we were climbing hills and walking among the trees.

After an hour or two, we came to open fields on the sides of gently rolling hills. We walked along beating the brush with a stick hoping to scare a rabbit or perhaps a pheasant. It was usually cold but I never minded. I was too excited with the hope of finding a rabbit. When we felt hungry, we stopped and built a fire. Then Uncle Carmine used to take out several links of fresh, sweet sausage from his pack and place them in a frying pan. Soon they were sizzling on the hot fire. As the aroma reached my nose, I became even more hungry. I could hardly wait. When the sausage was done, we put it between thick slices of my uncle's bread and ate. I can still smell that sausage, hear the crunch of the crusty bread as I bit into it, and taste the hot, juicy sausage.

In the afternoon we continued to hunt. When a rabbit started runnning in front of us, Uncle Carmine aimed for its hind legs and pulled the trigger. Once in a while he missed, but most of the time he didn't. We ran up to the rabbit quickly. Uncle Carmine picked it up. If it was still alive, he banged its head against a rock so that it would die quickly and not suffer. Then he put it in the big pocket in the back of his hunting jacket.

In the late afternoon when it was beginning to get dark, we headed back home. Sometimes we came back with two or three rabbits. Sometimes we came back empty-handed. But it didn't matter to me. The excitement for me was being out all day miles away from home walking with my uncle and his big gun. Even though I was much too small to carry a gun, I felt big and important when I was with my uncle.

Now I am grown up and Uncle Carmine is an old, old man. I haven't seen him in years because I live far away from him now. But I always remember him walking up the hill from the train station carrying two large round loaves of Italian bread wrapped in brown paper and tied together with a string.

ACTIVITY Write about a relative or friend that you are especially close to now or were close to when you were younger. Write about specific things that you used to do or do now with this relative or friend.

OPTIONAL ACTIVITIES

1. Questions for Comprehension   Either by yourself or with a partner answer the following questions to help you understand the story better.

Why did the story teller look forward to his Uncle Carmine's visits?
Why did the rabbit stew taste so good?
What were some of the things that the story teller enjoyed about hunting with Uncle Carmine?
Why didn't it matter to the story teller if they came back home empty-handed?
Why do you think that the story teller remembers his Uncle Carmine after all these years?

2. Retelling   After you have read about Uncle Carmine, tell the story again. Using your own words explain what the story says about him and the story teller.

CHI LIN'S ESCAPE TO FREEDOM

I had to get out. I couldn't stay in my country any longer. A new government had taken control the year before and I hated it. If I stayed, I would join the antigovernment movement, and sooner or later the soldiers would kill me or put me in prison. No, I had to leave. I had to be free.

One night while my parents, brothers and sisters were sleeping, I got up and left the house. I couldn't tell them where I was going, but it was so painful to leave them without saying goodbye. I walked until daylight, then hid under a tree and slept. When night came again, I got up and continued walking. I travelled this way for three weeks, walking at night and sleeping in caves or under trees during the day. I didn't want to meet anyone who might recognize me. And I was afraid to be seen by the police or soldiers who constantly patrolled the countryside.

I had very little to eat. Sometimes I found some wild fruit; other times some vegetables growing on farmland. Once I killed a chicken. But often I went to sleep hungry. I was becoming weak, but, when I thought of the freedom that waited for me on the other side of the river, I found new strength and I kept going.

Finally, on one very dark night I came to the river. Hearing it before I could see it, I began to run toward it. Suddenly I stopped and didn't move. I heard dogs barking. A patrol was coming along the river bank. Maybe the dogs would sense me. I quickly hid behind some bushes, afraid to move or even breathe. They came closer. I could see three dogs and a half dozen solders. Suddenly the dogs stopped and began sniffing the air. One of the soldiers looked toward the bushes where I was hiding. My heart was pounding. I was sure they would discover me. But then the dogs started moving again and the patrol passed by.

I waited until I couldn't hear the barking of the dogs any longer. Then I waded into the river and swam to the other side.

ACTIVITY Write about your decision to leave your native country.

What were the circumstances of your life in your native country that made you decide to leave?

Describe your departure. Was it easy or difficult for you to leave?

PAPA

Papa was coming. From the yard we could see him on his burro slowly coming up the road. The girls ran to meet him, their mother and I following. When he saw us, he waved, stopped the burro and waited. As we approached he lifted up his granddaughters one by one and hugged them warmly. Then it was his daughter Rosa's turn. The joy of seeing them again after so many months lit up his face. Finally a handshake for me as Rosa introduced me. Then, one of the girls leading the burro, we walked back up the road to the house, Papa speaking quietly with Rosa all the while. As we went I couldn't help notice his jet black hair, his deeply tanned skin and his muscular build. But what attracted me most were his eyes, black but clear. It wasn't until later that I became aware of what I was seeing in those beautiful eyes.

Back home we sat down to dinner in the rapidly descending darkness. The meal—simple but delicious—reflected the simplicity and poverty of country people like Papa and his family. I spoke of my work as a teacher back in the United States. Papa in a quiet, untroubled voice spoke of his work in the fields as a sugar cane cutter. He worked seven days a week. From 7:00 in the morning 'til 7:00 at night he cut the cane with his machete under the tropical sun. He had to rise at 5:00 each morning to begin a long, slow journey to the fields on the hard back of his burro. His pay was very low. He didn't say so, but it was clear that he barely made enough to provide the necessities for his wife and younger children.

After supper Rosa, her younger sister, Papa and I played dominoes by lantern light and shared a bottle of good island rum that we had brought for Papa. His clear eyes laughed often in the lantern light. Our eyes often met and I unashamedly stared into his, fascinated.

The time to leave arrived too quickly. Papa and Mama both said that they were honored to have had me as their guest and they hoped that I had enjoyed their hospitality. I assured them that I had enjoyed myself very much and thanked them. As I shook Papa's hand "goodbye," I looked one final time into his eyes. Then we left.

On the way back to Santiago I said very little to Rosa. I was thinking about Papa, trying to understand why he fascinated me. Finally it came to me. What I saw in Papa's eyes was peace. Papa was at peace with himself and his world. Even though he had to work incredibly hard and was incredibly poor, he had accepted all this as what was meant to be for him. He had found peace in the simplicity of his life and in his acceptance of it.

I began to think about my own life. I, a sophisticated, well-educated teacher from a big city with enough money to live well, had not found this inner peace. All my sophistication, all my education and all my money could not bring it to me. I had been looking for it for many years but had not found it, had not even known how to find it. So Papa who had nothing was richer than I who had a lot.

Then I began to see that things were backwards. Papa had said that he was honored to have me as his guest. But it should have been the other way around. I should have been the one honored to have met this simple man.

At the end of the summer I flew back to New York. Rosa stayed on her beautiful island with her children. I don't know if I will ever return. But whether or not I ever see Papa again, I know that I will never forget him.

ACTIVITY Write about someone (not related to you) you met sometime who was or is important to you in some way.

MY GRANDMA'S HOUSE

When I came home from school each day as a child, I grabbed a handful of cookies or a box of raisins to eat and ran up to my grandma's house. Her house was a half mile from where I lived.

It was an old house built on a hill. The outside was painted yellow and green. It was difficult to see from the road because it was surrounded by pine trees. To reach the house you had to walk up a long driveway. When I went there in the spring or summer, Grandma was always working in her garden so I didn't bother to go inside. Instead I climbed the stone steps in back of the house and walked along the path until I found her bent over her plants. Grandma was always glad to see me because I was her favorite grandson and also because I helped her do the things that were important to her. She was getting old so each spring I dug the garden for her and helped her plant. We planted rows and rows of tomatoes, corn, green peppers, string beans, radishes and many other kinds of vegetables.

Each day after we finished working in the garden, we went inside the house. It was warm and friendly inside especially in the kitchen. It was a large kitchen, filled with all the pots, pans, jars, bottles and other things Grandma needed to bake home-made bread, make noodles for soup, and preserve some of the vegetables that came from the garden. While I sat at the kitchen table and watched, Grandma cooked dinner for my aunt and uncle who still lived with her. She was a great cook. I can never forget the enormous meals she prepared for the entire family on holidays.

On some days when I got tired of watching Grandma cook, I picked up a watering can from the floor next to the sink, filled it and went to the front porch. Grandma kept her plants there because it faced west and had many large windows. She had dozens of plants, some big, some small, all lined up on tables in front of the windows. She loved plants and she taught me to love them too. She said that plants and flowers were given to us by God to make our lives more beautiful. I watered the plants, giving some a lot of water and others only a little as Grandma had taught me to do.

By the time I returned to the kitchen it was filled with the rich smells of the evening meal. Grandma always gave me a taste of whatever she was cooking.

At 7:00 I had to leave. My mother was waiting for me. I kissed Grandma goodbye, promising to return the next day. Then I walked down the driveway past the tall pine trees and went home.

Grandma died when I was sixteen. My aunt and uncle sold the house and moved away. Now many years later the house looks very different. The pine trees are gone and the house is painted blue. There is a small swimming pool in the back where the garden used to be. But whenever I drive by, I always remember the house as it was when Grandma lived there.

ACTIVITY   Write about a place that had some special meaning for you in the past or has some special meaning for you now.

PICTURE STORIES

PICTURE STORY NO. 1

ACTIVITY Charles and Marsha have been friends for two years. They have just met on the street. Something is wrong and they are talking about it. Write their conversation. Give the story a title.

PICTURE STORY NO. 2

ACTIVITY Jose and Ramon are sitting at the table. Lisa is standing at the bar with her arms folded. Tell a story about them. Give your story a title.

PICTURE STORY NO. 3

ACTIVITY Write about this man. Who is he? What is he thinking about? Give the story a title.

PICTURE STORY NO. 4

ACTIVITY Write about this girl. Where is she? What is she doing? Why? Give the story a title.

MODEL SENTENCES

SIMPLE PRESENT   Compare these sentences with those you used in your own writing.

The super is twenty-five years old.

He is not (isn't) an old man.

He has a large family.

He does not (doesn't) have a large family.

He lives in the basement.

He doesn't live in the building.

He works very hard.

Harry's neighbors are very friendly.

They are not (aren't) very friendly.

His coworkers like him.

His friends often visit him.

They usually do not (don't) visit him.

She is from the Dominican Republic.
She comes from Puerto Rico.
She lives with her family.

I want to get married.
I am (I'm) tired of arguing with you.
I have big plans for you.
I know what you are (you're) going to say.
I want you to listen to me.
I'm in love.
I would (I'd) like to tell you something.
I think you're wrong.

I don't want to be a lawyer.
I don't want you to take a job.
I'm not happy.
I don't think you understand.
I don't care.

You're old-fashioned.
You always tell me what to do.

You don't understand.
You're not interested in my feelings.

It is (It's) usually late when she gets home.

It doesn't matter.
It isn't a good job.

There is (There's) a sign in the window.

There isn't anyone else in the store.

There are many customers.

There aren't many customers.

Most Americans are friendly.
They usually try to help.
There is a lot of crime in big cities.

It is easy to get into school.

Most Americans aren't rich.
They don't often bother you.
There isn't much opportunity if you don't speak English.
It isn't easy to get a good job.

PRESENT CONTINUOUS   Compare these sentences to those you used in your own writing.

I am (I'm) feeling fine.
I'm listening to music.

Everyone is doing the same thing.
It is (It's) snowing now.
I'm taking English.

I'm going out to dinner tonight.
I'm enjoying myself.

I'm not feeling too good.
I'm not doing anything special right now.
My father isn't working today.
It isn't raining right now.
I'm not taking English next semester.

I'm not having a good time.

There are some things bothering me.
There is a picture hanging on the wall.
The girl is looking at someone.
She is thinking of something.
She is leaning against the counter.

There aren't many things happening right now.
There isn't anyone else working there.
She isn't looking at anything in particular.
She isn't smiling.
She isn't trying to sell anything.

PAST AND PAST CONTINUOUS   Compare these sentences to those you used in your own writing.

I was in my house
I called the police.
He was scared.
He started running.

I wasn't home that night.
I didn't know what to do.
He wasn't there.
He didn't start.

She went to a private school.
She was a good student.

She didn't go.
She wasn't happy.

It started raining.
It was a dark night.

It didn't start on time.
It wasn't warm enough.

We were frightened.
We did it carefully.
They were happy together.
They looked for shelter.

We weren't comfortable.
We didn't do it very well.
They weren't very happy.
They didn't look around.

I was walking home.
He was shouting for help.
She was unpacking the
    basket.
It was raining hard.
We were dancing together.
They were lying on the beach.

I wasn't watching.
He wasn't looking at me.
She wasn't feeling good.

It wasn't raining anymore.
We weren't trying to do it.
They weren't sleeping.

FUTURE Compare these phrases and sentences to those you used in your own writing.

I will get married to ...
I will marry a ...
You will have ...

You will not (won't) ...

I will work ...
I will make a lot of money.
You will start a business.

You will study accounting.
I will study to be an
    accountant.
You will major in accounting.

You will have good health.
I will live to be ninety
    (years old).

You will live happily.
You will be happy.

You are going to ...

You are not (aren't) going
    to ...
I won't ...

I will buy ...

I am going to ...

PRESENT PERFECT AND PRESENT PERFECT CONTINU-OUS Compare these phrases and sentences to those you used in your own writing.

I have (I've) lived in ____ since 1975.

I have not (haven't) been home for a long time.

I've been working at that job for ten years.

I haven't been sleeping well recently.

I've thought of that.
I've dreamt of your becoming...
I've been thinking of doing it for some time.
I've been dreaming about that for years.

In 1965 we moved to ____, where I've spent most of my life.

I've made many friends since coming here.

I haven't made many friends yet.

I've grown into a more mature person.

I've decided to do it.

I haven't asked you to do that.

I've already made up my mind.

I haven't made up my mind yet.

I've told you what I'm going to do.

I've planned your future for you.

I haven't made any plans so far.

You've got to stop doing that.
She's been here for some time.
We've decided to get married.
They've been waiting a long time.

She hasn't been here long.
We haven't decided yet.
They haven't been waiting very long.

Questions	Answers
1. How long have you ... ?	I've been ... for a long time/a week/a month. I've been ... since Tuesday/1978
2. How often have you ... ?	I've ... many times/twice/ often.
3. Have you ever ... ?	No, I've never ... Yes, I have.
4. Where have you been ... ?	Recently/For the past month/ Lately I've been ...
5. Have you ... yet/lately/ within the past month?	No, I haven't ... yet/recently/ within the past six months. Yes, I've already ...

INFINITIVES Compare these sentences and phrases to those you used in your own writing.

They started to investigate.
They told him to put ...
They want to keep guns ...
They tried to run and hide.
They didn't know what to do.
They decided to come.
They can't afford to pay the rent.
They are planning to go.
I want to thank you ...
She asked him to give ...

I am here to tell you ...
They wear suits and long dresses to go to weddings.
It is not easy to get a job.
You can get a job as a salesman to speak Spanish to the customers.
They took three hours to put out the fire.
I used the telephone to call ...
They have plans to go to Europe.

MODALS Compare these sentences and phrases to those you used in your own writing.

I can make decisions by myself.
I hope that you can continue your studies.
She wants to know if I can help her.
You can get married if you want to.

You can't do that to me.
I can't do anything about it.
I know I can't rely on you.

She waited until I could leave.
I wish I could be like her.
She made me see that I could become a better person.

They couldn't call.
They couldn't figure out what was happening.

I would like . . .
I said I would call.
They said they would try.
I thought I would die.

You wouldn't dare . . .
It wouldn't look good.

He should be here soon.
You should listen to me.
You should have followed my advice.

You shouldn't talk like that.

You may be right.
It may/might rain tomorrow.

They may/might not get here on time.

You may do what you like.

You may not come here anymore.

QUESTIONS   Compare these questions to those you used in your own writing.

Is she from a good family?

Is that what you want to do?   Isn't that what you want?

Are you serious?

Are you going to disobey
 me?   Aren't you going to listen to
 me?

Was that what you wanted to
 tell me?   Wasn't that what we
 decided?

Were you telling me the
 truth?   Weren't you telling me the
 truth?

Do you want to make me look
 foolish?   Don't you want to get
 married?

Does she come from a good
 family?   Doesn't he have anything
 better to do?

Did you want to tell me
 something?   Didn't we agree to that?

Has something happened?

Have you thought this over
 carefully?   Haven't you been happy?

Will you let me do it?   Won't you listen to me?

Would you please do this for
 me?

Can you tell me why?   Can't you see it's a mistake?

Who is she?
Who are they?

What's wrong with you?
What are you talking about?
What do you want to do?
What did you say?
What about our plans?

Why are you doing this?
Why don't you want to do it?
Why won't you let me do it?

Where are you planning to live?
Where did you meet her?
Where will you work?
Where have you been?

When do you want to start?
When will you do this?

How is business?
How are you doing?

DIRECT AND INDIRECT SPEECH   Compare these sentences to those you used in your own writing.

Direct Speech	*Indirect Speech*
I asked Bill, "Who is she?"	I asked Bill who she was.
"What is she doing here?" I asked him.	I asked him what she was doing there.
He said, "She is . . ."	He said (that) she was . . .
"It's nothing," he replied.	He replied that it was nothing.
He said, "I was drunk."	He said (that) he had been drunk.
I said to Bill, "I want . . ."	I told Bill (that) I wanted . . .
"I think . . .," I told him.	I told him (that) I thought . . .

He said, "You will live to be one-hundred."	He said I would live to be one-hundred.
"You will marry soon."	He told me (that) I would marry soon.
"People will remember you for ___ ."	He said that people would remember me for ___ .
"I can't believe it," I screamed.	I screamed that I couldn't believe it.
"I never thought it would be me," I told him.	I told him that I never thought it would be me.
"I like this country very much."	She said that she liked this country very much.
	She said that she likes this country very much.
	She says that she likes this country very much.
"I don't like this school."	He said that he didn't like this school.
	He said that he doesn't like this school.
	He says that he doesn't like this school.